Start TO Finish
Second Series

FROM Acorn TO Oak Tree

EMMA CARLSON BERNE

LERNER PUBLICATIONS Minneapolis

To Martha Warshaw,
one of the great nature lovers
of my childhood

Lerner Publications Company
A division of Lerner Publishing Group, Inc.
241 First Avenue North
Minneapolis, MN 55401 USA

For reading levels and more information, look up this title at www.lernerbooks.com.

Library of Congress Cataloging-in-Publication Data

Names: Berne, Emma Carlson, author.
Title: From acorn to oak tree / Emma Carlson Berne.
Other titles: Start to finish (Minneapolis, Minn.).
    Second series.
Description: Minneapolis : Lerner Publications, [2017] |
    Series: Start to finish. Second series | Audience: Ages
    5-9. | Audience: K to grade 3. | Includes bibliographical
    references and index.
Identifiers: LCCN 2016037237 (print) | LCCN
    2016042353 (ebook) | ISBN 9781512434408
    (lb : alk. paper) | ISBN 9781512450927 (eb pdf)
Subjects: LCSH: Oak—Life cycles—Juvenile literature. |
    Acorns—Juvenile literature.
Classification: LCC QK495.F14 B47 2017 (print) |
    LCC QK495.F14 (ebook) | DDC 583/.46—dc23

LC record available at https://lccn.loc.gov/2016037237

Manufactured in the United States of America
3-45727-25383-5/2/2018

TABLE OF Contents

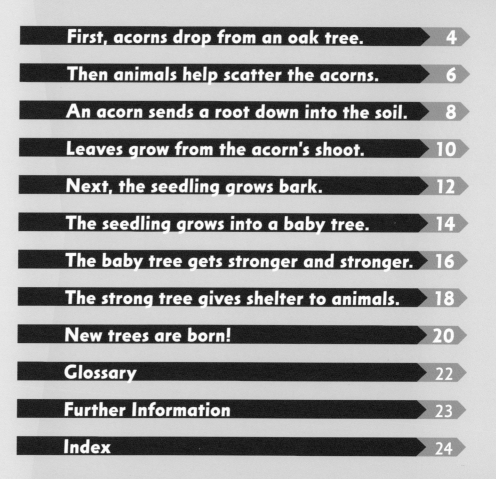

Oak trees stand tall. How do they grow?

3

First, acorns drop from an oak tree.

This happens in the fall. An acorn is an oak tree **nut**. A hard shell outside protects the soft inside. A tiny **germ** of a plant is inside waiting to sprout. An oak tree grows many acorns every year.

Then animals help scatter the acorns.

Some acorns sink into the ground where they fell. Animals such as squirrels and birds take other acorns away. They drop the acorns or bury them.

An acorn sends a root down into the soil.

The acorn **anchors** itself with the root. Spring comes and rain falls. Then the acorn shell cracks. A little **shoot** comes out of the shell. It starts reaching up to the sky.

Leaves grow from the acorn's shoot.

The acorn isn't a nut anymore. Now it is a **seedling**. The roots drink water from the soil. The leaves gather **nutrients** from the sun.

Next, the seedling grows bark.

The bark grows thicker. The seedling grows taller and stronger. Small branches and more leaves grow. Under the soil, the roots spread out.

The seedling grows into a baby tree.

The seedling becomes a **sapling**. The sapling is still a baby tree. It can't make acorns yet.

The baby tree gets stronger and stronger.

The sapling's bark grows thicker and tougher. The branches spread out more, and thick leaves wave in the air. The oak tree is a **mature** tree now.

The strong tree gives shelter to animals.

Squirrels nest in the tree's branches. Birds may build nests there. And insects eat the tree's leaves. Oak trees also give off good air for people and animals to breathe.

New trees are born!

The tree grows acorns, and the acorns fall off. The cycle starts all over. New oak trees bring new life to a forest.

Glossary

anchors: holds on tightly so something can't move away

germ: the basis or beginning of something

mature: grown-up

nut: a hard shell around a soft inside that can be eaten by animals and people. An oak tree nut, or acorn, grows into an oak tree.

nutrients: substances that plants, animals, and people need to live and grow

sapling: a young tree with a trunk that is 1 to 4 inches (2.5 to 10 centimeters) wide

seedling: a young plant that has just sprouted

shoot: the part of a new plant that is just beginning to grow above the ground

Further Information

Arbor Day Foundation: Life of a Tree
https://www.arborday.org/kids/carly/lifeofatree
Watch this interesting video to see how a tree grows.

Boothroyd, Jennifer. *Let's Visit the Deciduous Forest*. Minneapolis: Lerner Publications, 2017. Learn what's in a deciduous forest in this fun walk through a biome.

Kids.gov: Plants
https://kids.usa.gov/science/plants/index.shtml
Visit the US government's website just for kids to learn all about gardening, nature, and plants.

Pipe, Jim. *You Wouldn't Want to Live without Trees!* New York: Franklin Watts, 2016. Learn everything you've ever wanted to know about trees in this general fact guide.

Russo, Monica. *Treecology: 30 Activities and Observations for Exploring the World of Trees and Forests*. Chicago: Chicago Review Press, 2016. Take your knowledge outdoors with this activity book all about nature.

Index

Photo Acknowledgments
The images in this book are used with the permission of: © iStockphoto.com/kingjon, p. 1; © iStockphoto.com/DNY59, p. 3; © iStockphoto.com/Peter Topp Enge Jonasen, p. 5; © TessarTheTegu/Shutterstock.com, p. 7; © Vitalii Hulai/Shutterstock.com, p. 9; © James L. Amos/Science Source, p. 11; © Dmitrij Yakovets/Shutterstock.com, p. 13; © AJF natural collection/Alamy, p. 15; © iStockphoto.com/Alexey Romanov, p. 17; © Shico300/Dreamstime.com, p. 19.

Front cover: © iStockphoto.com/Whiteway.

Main body text set in Arta Std Book 20/26.
Typeface provided by International Typeface Corp.

LERNER
e
SOURCE

Expand learning beyond the printed book. Download free, complementary educational resources for this book from our website, www.lerneresource.com.